THE LITTLE BOOK OF
ZOO
JOKES

THIS IS A CARLTON BOOK

Published by The Carlton Publishing Group
20 Mortimer Street
London W1T 3JW
Text copyright © 2005 and 2008 EMAP
Design and layout copyright © 2008 Carlton Books

This book is sold subject to the condition that it
shall not, by way of trade or otherwise, be lent,
resold, hired out or otherwise circulated without the
publisher's prior written consent in any form of cover
or binding other than that in which it is published and
without a similar condition including this condition
being imposed upon the subsequent purchaser. All
rights reserved.

ISBN 978-1-84732-078-0

2 4 6 8 10 9 7 5 3 1

Printed in Singapore

The jokes in this book first appeared in
The Zoo Rude Jokes Book

THE LITTLE BOOK OF ZOO JOKES

CARLTON

Brought to you from the readers of ZOO magazine

Women's hormones

A woman goes to her doctor to complain about the side-effects of the testosterone pills he's given her.

She says, 'Doctor, I'm wondering if you got the dosage right. I've started growing hair in places I've never grown hair before.'

The doctor says, 'A little growth is a perfectly normal side-effect of testosterone. Just where has this happened?'

She says, 'On my balls.'

Man UTD stamps

The Post Office has recalled its Manchester United-themed stamps. People couldn't work out which side to spit on.

Ugliest in the land

Snow White, Tom Thumb and Quasimodo are sitting in a pub with their mates.

Snow White says, 'There's no doubt about it: I'm the fairest in the land.'

Tom Thumb says, 'There's no doubt about it: I'm the smallest in the land.'

Quasimodo says, 'There's no doubt about it: I'm the ugliest in the land.'

Their mates tell them to prove it by going to the magic all-knowing mirror. The three head off.

A few minutes later, the door of the pub bursts open and Snow White runs in and shouts, 'It's official – I'm the fairest in the land!'

Shortly afterwards, the door again bursts open and Tom Thumb runs in and shouts, 'It's official – I'm the smallest in the land!'

Five minutes later, the door gets kicked in and Quasimodo stomps through and bellows, 'Who the hell is Jade Goody?'

Pregnancy query

A woman goes to her doctor and says, 'Can you get pregnant from anal sex?'

The doctor says, 'Of course. Where do you think Leicester fans come from?'

Fiddling fun

Q. What do a Rubik's Cube and a penis have in common?
A. The longer you play with them, the harder they get.

Dying man

A bloke gets back from the doctor's one day and tells his wife he's only got 24 hours to live.

Wiping away her tears, he asks her to have sex with him. Of course, she agrees, and they make passionate love.

Six hours later, he says, 'Darling, now I have only 18 hours to live. Can we have sex again?' She agrees.

Later, he's getting into bed when he realises he now has only eight hours of life left.

He says, 'Darling? Please? Just one more time before I die.'

She agrees; then afterwards she rolls over and falls asleep.

He, however, hears the clock ticking, and he tosses and turns until he's down to only four more hours. He taps his wife on the shoulder to wake her up.

He says, 'Darling, I only have four hours left. Could we…?' His wife sits up abruptly and yells, 'Look, I have to get up in the morning – you don't.'

Pete and Bill

Q. What do you get if you cross Pete Doherty with Bill Oddie?
A. A quack addict.

Zebra

Q. What is a zebra?
A. Twenty-five sizes larger than an 'A' bra.

Dead dog

Q. What's the difference between a dead dog in the road and a dead Manchester United fan in the road?
A. The dog has skid marks in front of it.

Blonde's kids

A blonde goes to the council to register for child benefit.

'How many children?' asks the council worker.

'Ten,' says the blonde.

'Ten?' says the council worker. 'What are their names?'

'Wayne, Wayne, Wayne, Wayne, Wayne, Wayne, Wayne, Wayne, Wayne and Wayne.'

'Doesn't that get confusing?'

'No,' says the blonde. 'It's great, because if they're out playing in the street I just have to shout, "Wayne, your dinner's ready" or "Wayne, go to bed now" and they all do it.'

'But what if you want to speak to one individually?' asks the council worker.

'Easy,' says the blonde. 'I just use their surnames.'

Mafia and cunnilingus

Q. What do the Mafia and cunnilingus have in common?
A. One slip of the tongue and you're in deep shit.

Blonde's flowers

Two blondes meet up. The first one says, 'My boyfriend bought me a bunch of flowers on Friday evening. I had to keep my legs open all weekend.'

The other says, 'Why? Didn't you have a vase?'

Father's jobs

The teacher says, 'Let's discuss what your dads do for a living.'

Mary says, 'My dad is a lawyer. He puts bad guys in jail.'

Jack says, 'My dad is a doctor. He makes sick people better.'

Johnny doesn't raise his hand, so the teacher says, 'Johnny, what does your dad do?'

Johnny says, 'My dad's dead.'

The teacher says, 'I'm sorry to hear that. But what did he do before he died?'

Johnny says, 'He turned blue and shat on the carpet.'

Gay row

Did you hear about the two gay blokes who had a row in a pub?

They went outside to exchange blows.

Laura on top

Q. Why does Laura Bush have to go on top?
A. Because George W Bush always fucks up.

Chav's welsh query

Some chavs are driving through Wales.

As they approach Llanfairpwllgwyngyllgogerychwyrndrobwllllantysiliogogogoch, they start arguing about the pronunciation of the town's name. The row continues until lunchtime.

As they stand at the counter of the local restaurant, one chav says to the blonde serving girl, 'Before we order, could you settle an argument for us? Would you please pronounce where we are, very slowly?'

The blonde leans over the counter and says, 'Burrrrrrrrgerrrrrrr Kiiiiing.'

Tax inspector

At the end of the tax year, the Tax Office sends an inspector to audit the books of a synagogue. While he's checking the books, he says to the Rabbi, 'I notice you buy a lot of candles. What do you do with the candle drippings?'

The Rabbi says, 'We save them up and send them back to the candle-makers, and every now and then they send us a complete box of candles.'

The tax inspector says, 'What about all these matzo balls you buy? What do you do with the crumbs?'

The Rabbi says, 'We collect them and send them back to the manufacturers, and every now and then they send a complete box of matzo balls.'

The tax inspector says, 'And what do you do with all the leftover foreskins from the circumcisions you perform?' The Rabbi says, 'Here, too, we do not waste. We save up all the foreskins and send them to the Tax Office, and about once a year they send us a complete dick.'

Macho woman

Q. How do you spot a macho woman?
A. She's rolling her own tampons.

Jacko race

Q. Why can you always win a race with Michael Jackson?
A. Because he likes to come in a little behind.

Types of breasts

One day, at the dinner table, a son asks his father, 'Dad, how many kinds of breasts are there?'

The father says, 'Son, there are three types. In her twenties, a woman's breasts are like melons, round and firm. In her thirties to forties, they're like pears, still nice but drooping a bit. After 50, they're like onions.'

'Onions?' says the son.

'Yes, you see them and they make you cry.'

This infuriates his mum and daughter, so the daughter says, 'Mum, how many kinds of penises are there?'

The mother looks at her husband and says, 'Well, dear, a man goes through three phases. In his twenties, his penis is like an oak, mighty and hard. In his thirties to forties, it's like a birch, flexible but reliable. After his fifties, it's like a Christmas tree.'

'A Christmas tree?' says the daughter.

'Yes, dead from the root up and the balls are for decoration only.'

Poisoned penis

Two blokes are walking through the jungle when the first is bitten on the penis by a snake. Quickly, the second bloke rings the emergency services on his mobile.

'My friend's been bitten by a snake,' he cries. 'What can I do?'

The operator says, 'Is it a poisonous snake?'

'Yes, a tiger snake,' says the second bloke.

'Then you must immediately suck the poison out, or your friend will be dead within an hour.'

The second bloke hangs up and says, 'Sorry, mate – he says you'll be dead within an hour.'

Wives and vacuum cleaners

Q. What do your wife and a vacuum cleaner have in common?
A. After a year they stop sucking and start whining.

Swallowed a condom

Victoria Beckham phones the doctor in a panic late one night.

She says, 'Doctor, you've got to come over. David's just swallowed a condom.'

The doctor rushes to get his things together when the phone rings. It's Victoria again.

She says, 'Don't worry, Doc, there's no need to come round. We've found another one.'

Girlfriend and wife

Q. What's the difference between a girlfriend and a wife?
A. About two stone.

Your mum

Two blokes are in a pub.
One says to the other, 'I shagged your mum.'
The other doesn't reply.
Again the first one shouts, 'I shagged your mum.'
The whole pub turns round to watch.
The other bloke says, 'Go home, Dad, you're drunk.'

Whales

Two whales overturn a ship using their blowholes.

'Can we eat the crew?' asks one.

'No,' says the other. 'I do blow-jobs, but I don't swallow seamen.'

Wearing the trousers

Dave is about to marry Davina and his father takes him to one side. He says, 'When I married your mother, the first thing I did when we got home was take off my trousers. I gave them to your mother and told her to put them on. When she did, they were enormous on her and she said to me that she couldn't possibly wear them. I said, "Of course they're too big. I wear the trousers in this family and I always will." Ever since that day, we've never had a single problem.'

Dave takes his father's advice and as soon as he gets Davina alone after the wedding he does the same thing: takes off his trousers, gives them to Davina and tells her to put them on. Davina says the trousers are too big and that she couldn't possibly wear them. Dave says, 'Exactly. I wear the trousers in this relationship and I always will. I don't want you to forget that.'

Davina pauses, removes her knickers and gives them to Dave. She says, 'Try these on.' He does, but they're too small.

He says, 'I can't possibly get into your knickers.'

She says, 'Exactly. And if you don't change your attitude, you never will.'

Want a watch

Little Johnny sees that his friend at school has a new watch, so he asks him how he got it.

His friend says, 'I waited until I heard the bedsprings squeaking in my parents' bedroom and then I ran in. My father gave me a watch to get rid of me.'

So Johnny goes home and waits until he hears the bedsprings squeaking and then runs into his parents' bedroom.

His father yells, 'What's up?'

Johnny says, 'I wanna watch!'

His father says, 'Well, then, sit down and shut up!'

Smoking

Q. What do you do if your girlfriend starts smoking?
A. Slow down and use some lubricant.

Nympho parrot

Did you hear about the nymphomaniac parrot?
She liked a cock or two.

Biggest drawback

Q. What's the biggest drawback in the jungle?
A. An elephant's foreskin.

Substitute priest

A priest has been in the confessional all day without a break. He's desperate to take a dump, but people keep coming to confess and he hates to leave. Eventually, he peers out of his cubicle and signals the janitor to come over. He asks the janitor to cover for him, gives him the confessions book, then rushes off in the direction of the toilet.

The janitor is bewildered, but he goes into the confessional and sits down.

A woman on the other side says, 'Bless me, Father, for I have sinned. I cheated on my husband.'

The janitor scans through the book until he finds

'Adultery'. He tells the woman to say 50 Hail Marys and wash in holy water.

Next comes a man who says, 'Bless me, Father, for I have sinned. I had oral sex with another man.'

The janitor hunts through the book, but he can't find a penance for oral sex.

He leans out of the confessional and whispers to an altar boy, 'What does the priest give for oral sex?'

The boy says, 'Five quid and a chocolate bar.'

Jacko and homework

Q. What do Michael Jackson and homework have in common?
A. They're a pain in the arse to kids.

Women and computers

Q. What's the difference between a woman and a computer?
A. A woman won't accept a three-and-a-half-inch floppy.

Owen on the pull

Michael Owen walks into a nightclub, goes straight up to a girl, starts feeling her tits and says, 'Get your coat, sexy, you're coming home with me.'

The girl says, 'You're a little forward.'

Woman's pains

A woman visits her doctor to complain about strange abdominal pains. He examines her and says, 'I hope you're looking forward to many sleepless nights because of crying and nappy-changing.'

'Why,' says the woman, 'am I pregnant?'

'No,' says the doctor, 'you've got bowel cancer.'

Pregnant teen

An 18-year-old girl tells her mother she's missed her period for two months. Worried, the mother buys a pregnancy test kit. The result shows that the girl is pregnant.

Furious, the mother yells, 'Who was the pig that did this to you?'

The girl picks up the phone and makes a call. Half an hour later a Ferrari stops outside. A man in a very expensive suit climbs out and enters the house.

He sits in the living room with the father, the mother and the girl, and says, 'Your daughter has informed me of the problem. I can't marry her because of my family situation, but I'll take charge. If a girl is born, I will bequeath her two shops, a townhouse, a beach villa and a £1,000,000 bank account. If a boy is born, my legacy will be a couple of factories and a £2,000,000 bank account. If it's twins, a factory and £1,000,000 each. However, if there is a miscarriage, what do you suggest I do?'

The father places a hand firmly on the man's shoulder and says, 'Fuck her again.'

Parachutes

George W Bush, the Pope and a little boy are on the same plane. Suddenly the engines fail and the captain says, 'We're going to crash. Grab a parachute and escape while you can.'

The three of them rush over to the parachutes – but find there are only two.

Bush grabs one, opens the door and jumps out, shouting, 'I'm too important to die!'

The Pope and the little boy look at each other.

The Pope says, 'Little boy, I've had a good long life and I'm sure I'll be going to a better place. You take the parachute.'

The little boy says, 'It's OK, you have it – and I'll have the second one. That tit Bush took my rucksack.'

Nun's punishment

Three men are travelling and looking for a place to stay. Eventually they come across a convent and ask the Mother Superior if they can stay the night.

She says, 'If I catch you looking at my nuns in the showers, I'll have to cut your dicks off.'

Sure enough, they get caught, and she asks the first man, 'What's your job?'

'A butcher.'

'Then I'll cut your dick off with a knife.'

The second guy says he's a joiner, so the nun says, 'I'll cut yours off with a saw.'

Finally she turns to the third man and says the same, to which he replies, 'I'm a lollipop man. What are you gonna do – suck it?'

Whiff of defeat

Q. Why do Spurs fans smell?
A. So the blind can hate them as well.

Look before you leap

Q. What have a bungee jump and a blow-job from an 80-year-old got in common?
They're great if you don't look down.

Chav's top tipple

Q. What's a chav girl's favourite wine?
A. 'Aw, go on, take me to Lakeside, please, please, go on, take me…'

Quiet one

During sex, a bloke says to his wife, 'How come you never tell me when you have an orgasm?'

She says, 'You're never home when it happens.'

Sex drug

A bloke walks into a chemist and says to the assistant, 'I have three girls coming over tonight. I've never had three at once, so I need something to keep me horny.'

The chemist gives him a box of mysterious pills marked with an 'X' and says, 'Here, if you eat these you'll be rock-hard for 12 hours.'

The bloke says, 'Brilliant! Give me three boxes.'

The next day, the bloke walks into the same chemist and pulls down his trousers. The assistant looks in horror as he notices the man's cock is black and blue, with skin hanging off in places.

The man says, 'Give me a bottle of Deep Heat.'

The assistant says, 'Deep Heat? You're not going to put Deep Heat on that, are you?'

The man says, 'No, it's for my arms – the girls didn't show up.'

Cardboard box

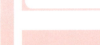

Q. What's worse than a cardboard box?
A. Paper tits.

Lucky lad

Q. What do you call a Welshman with a sheep under each arm?
A. A pimp.

Ugly wife

A husband and wife are getting ready for bed. The wife is standing in front of a full-length mirror taking a long hard look at herself.

'You know, dear,' she says, 'I look in the mirror and I see an old woman. My face is wrinkled, my boobs barely clear my waist and my arse is sagging. I've got fat legs and my arms are flabby. Tell me something positive to make me feel better about myself.'

He says, 'Well, there's nothing wrong with your eyesight.'

Scottish woman

A Scottish woman walks in on her husband wanking into a welly.

She yells, 'Stop fucking aboot!'

Bush's burger

George W Bush strides into a library and shouts, 'Hi, ma'am! I'd like a burger and fries please!'

The librarian says, 'For fuck's sake, you idiot, this is a library!'

'Sorry,' says Bush, and whispers, 'I'd like a burger and fries, please.'

Pork pies and hand-jobs

A bloke's walking down the street when he sees a sign in the window of a local shop: 'Pork pies 50p, hand-jobs £1.'

He goes in and sees the most beautiful girl behind the counter.

He says, 'Are you the girl who gives hand-jobs for a pound?'

She nods.

He says, 'Wash your hands, then; I want a pork pie.'

Blue and orange

Q. What's blue and orange and lies at the bottom of a swimming pool?
A. A baby with burst armbands.

Woman's waist

Q. Why is the space between a woman's breasts and hips called a waist?
A. Because you could fit another pair of tits there.

Fartball

An old man and his wife are in bed. After lying there for a few minutes, the old man farts and shouts, 'Goal!'

His wife says, 'What the hell was that?'

The old man says, 'I'm ahead one-nil.'

A few minutes later, the wife lets one go and shouts, 'Goal! One-all!'

After another ten minutes, the old man farts again. 'Goal! Two-one!'

The wife quickly farts again and shouts, 'Goal! Two-all!'

Not to be outdone, the old man strains as hard as

he can to squeeze out the winning fart. Unfortunately, he tries too hard and shits the bed.

His wife says, 'What the hell was that?'

The old man says, 'Half-time. Swap sides…'

Chemist and condoms

A girl asks her boyfriend to come over on Friday night and have dinner with her parents, and says that after dinner she'd like to have sex with him for the first time.

The boy is ecstatic, but he's never had sex before, so he goes to the chemist to get some condoms.

The chemist asks the boy how many condoms he'd like to buy: a three-pack, a six-pack or a 10-pack. The boy chooses the 10-pack because he reckons he'll be busy.

That night, the boy shows up at the girl's house and meets his girlfriend at the door.

She says, 'Oh, I'm so excited that you're going to meet my parents. Come in!'

The boy goes inside and is taken to the dinner table, where the girl's parents are seated. The boy decides to say grace and bows his head.

Ten seconds pass and the boy is still deep in prayer, with his head down.

Twenty seconds pass and still no movement from the boy.

Finally, after the boy has spent a minute with his head down, his girlfriend leans over and whispers, 'I had no idea you were this religious.'

The boy whispers back, 'I had no idea your dad was a chemist.'

Design triumph

Q. Who helped God design woman?
A. The council – who else would put a playground next to a shithole?

Sheep in long grass

Q. How does a Welshman find a sheep in long grass?
A. Irresistible.

Wives and jobs

Q. What's the difference between your wife and your job?
A. After 10 years your job still sucks.

Leeds fly past

Q. What do you call 20 Leeds fans sky-diving?
A. Diarrhoea.

Cock clock

A cowboy is riding on the plains. He comes across a Red Indian boy lying naked on his back with a huge erection.

The cowboy says, 'What the hell are you doing?' The Indian looks at the shadow of his cock and says, 'It's 1pm.'

The cowboy rides on. Soon he runs into another Red Indian. He too is lying on his back naked with a huge erection.

The cowboy says, 'What the hell are you doing?'

The Indian looks at the shadow of his cock and says, 'It's 2.30pm.'

The cowboy rides on.

Later he comes upon a third Red Indian. This one is lying on his back naked, masturbating.

The cowboy says, 'Christ! What the hell are you doing?'

The Indian says, 'I'm winding my watch.'

Sex disease

Big Gay Glenn goes to the doctor and has some tests. The doctor comes back and says, 'Glenn, I'm not going to beat about the bush. You have AIDS.'

Glenn is devastated. 'Doctor, what can I do?'

'Eat one sausage, one head of cabbage, 20 unpeeled carrots drenched in hot sauce, 10 Jalapeno peppers, 40 walnuts, 40 peanuts, half a box of Grape Nuts and top it off with a gallon of prune juice.'

Glenn asks, 'Will that cure me, Doctor?'

The doctor says, 'No, but it should leave you with a better understanding of what your arse is for.'

Miss piggy

Q. Why can't Miss Piggy count to 70?
A. She gets a frog in her throat at 69.

Brothel parrot

A woman goes into a pet shop and decides to buy a parrot. The assistant says, 'I must warn you: this parrot used to live in a brothel.' The woman is concerned, but decides to buy it anyway.

When the woman gets home, she leaves the parrot in the lounge and waits for the reaction from her family.

Her son comes into the room. The parrot says, 'Who's a pretty boy, then?'

The woman thinks, 'That's OK.'

Then her daughter walks in. The parrot says, 'Hello, sexy.'

The woman thinks, 'Well, that's not too bad. I shouldn't have worried.'

Then her husband gets back from work. The parrot says, 'Hi, John, not seen you since last week.'

Marriage

Q. What do tornadoes and marriage have in common?
A. They both start with a lot of blowing and in the end you lose your house.

Glory, glory

A woman visits her doctor and says, 'I keep hearing the sound of "Glory, glory Man United" coming from my crotch!'

The doctor says, 'Don't worry, a lot of twats sing that.'

Persian rugs

A lady walks into a shop which sells Persian rugs. She spots the perfect rug and walks over to inspect it. As she bends over to feel its texture, she farts loudly. Embarrassed, she looks around to see if anyone has noticed. Standing nearby is a salesman.

He says, 'Good day, madam. How may we help you?'

Uncomfortably, she says, 'What's the price of this rug?'

He says, 'Madam, if you farted just touching it, you'll shit yourself when you hear the price.'

Ultimate rejection

Q. What's the ultimate rejection?
A. Your hand falling asleep as you masturbate.

Tough prostitute

A hard bloke walks into a brothel holding two unopened bottles of beer and growls, 'I'm looking for the roughest, toughest prostitute in town.'

The pimp says, 'No problem. She's upstairs, second room on the right.'

The hard bloke stomps up the stairs, kicks the door open and bellows, 'I'm looking for the roughest, toughest prostitute in town.'

The woman inside the room says, 'You found her!'

She strips naked, bends over and grabs her ankles.

The hard man says, 'How do you know I want that position first?'

The prostitute says, 'I don't. I just thought you might want to open those beers first.'

Blind nudist

Q. How do you find a blind man in a nudist colony?
A. It's not hard.

Chav wants a job

A chav walks into the Jobcentre, marches up to the counter and says, 'Hi, I'm looking for a job.'

The man behind the counter replies, 'Well, we've just got a listing from a millionaire who wants a chauffeur/bodyguard for his nymphomaniac daughter. You'll have to drive around in a Mercedes, uniform provided. Because of the long hours, meals will be provided, and you'll also be required to escort the young lady on her holidays. The salary is £200k.'

The chav says, 'You're bullshitting me!'

The man says, 'Well, you started it!'

Anal deodorant

A blonde walks into a chemist's and asks the assistant for some anal deodorant. The chemist, a little bemused, explains to the woman that they don't sell anal deodorant and never have done. Unfazed, the blonde assures the chemist she's often bought the stuff from this shop and would like some more.

'I'm sorry,' says the chemist. 'Do you have the container it came in?'

'Yes,' says the blonde, producing it from her handbag.

The chemist says, 'But this is just a normal stick of underarm deodorant.'

The blonde replies, 'But the label says, "To apply, push up bottom."'

Bullets

A pregnant woman is walking down the street when she gets caught up in a bank robbery getaway and is shot three times in the stomach. Miraculously, she makes a full recovery and gives birth to triplets: one boy and two girls.

One day, about 16 years later, one of the girls runs to the mother in tears.

The woman says, 'What's the matter?'

The daughter sobs, 'I went to the toilet and a bullet came out.'

A couple of weeks later, the second girl runs in crying, after exactly the same thing has happened to her.

Another week later, the boy runs to his mother and, like his sisters, he's in tears.

His mother says, 'Let me guess: you went to the toilet and a bullet came out?'

The boy says, 'No, I was having a wank and I shot the dog!'

Stuffed full

John goes to the doctors and says, 'Doctor, you've got to help me – I just can't get a hard-on.'

So the doctor examines his cock and says, 'Your cock muscles are too weak. We're going to have to take the muscles from an elephant's cock and graft them on to your penis.'

John's desperate for sex, so he agrees. After the op, John goes out on a dinner date with a new girl.

But half-way through the meal, his cock starts to feel strange and uncomfortably big, so to release the strain he unzips his flies under the table.

Suddenly his cock springs out of his trousers, grabs

a bun from the next table and shoots back into his trousers with it.

His date is stunned and says, 'Christ, you've got a huge cock. Can you do that again?'

John replies, 'Well, I could try, but I don't think I can fit another bun up my arse.'

Lesbian periods

Q. What do you call two lesbians on their period?
A. Finger painting.

Angels

A girl is standing at the gates of heaven when she hears screams of pain coming from inside.

She says to St Peter, 'What's going on?'

He says, 'That's the sound of new angels getting big holes drilled into their backs for their wings and small holes drilled into their heads for their halos.'

She says, 'Heaven sounds terrible. I think I'd rather go to hell.'

St Peter says, 'In hell, you'll be constantly raped and sodomised.'

She says, 'That's OK, I've already got holes for that.'

Irishman falls flat

An Irishman has been drinking at a pub all night. The landlord finally says that the bar is closing. But when the Irishman stands up to leave, he falls flat on his face. He tries to stand again, with the same result. He decides to crawl outside and get some fresh air to sober him up. Once outside, he tries to stand up – but again falls flat on his face. So he decides to crawl home. When he arrives at the door, he tries to stand up – but again falls flat on his face. He crawls through the door and into his bedroom.

When he reaches his bed, he tries once again to stand up. This time he manages to pull himself upright, but immediately he collapses onto the duvet and falls asleep.

He's awakened the next morning by his wife shouting, 'So, you've been out drinking again!'

He says, 'What makes you say that?'

She says, 'The pub called – you left your wheelchair there again.'

Public schoolboy

Q. How do you know if a public schoolboy is a gentleman?
A. He'll take a girl out five times before shagging her younger brother.

Blinking

Q. Why don't women blink during foreplay?
A. They don't have time.

Liverpool class

A teacher starts a new job at a school on Merseyside and, trying to make a good impression on her first day, explains to her class that she is a Liverpool fan. She asks her students to raise their hands if they, too, are Liverpool fans.

Everyone in the class raises their hand except one little girl. The teacher looks at her and says, 'Mary, why didn't you raise your hand?'

Mary says, 'Because I'm not a Liverpool fan.'

The teacher says, 'If you're not a Liverpool fan, who are you a fan of?'

Mary says, 'I'm a Manchester United fan.'

The teacher says, 'Why?'

Mary says, 'Because my mum is a United fan and my dad is a United fan, so I'm a United fan, too.'

The teacher says, 'That's no reason for you to be a United fan. You don't have to be just like your parents all the time. What if your mum was a prostitute and your dad was a drug addict – what would you be then?'

Mary says, 'A Liverpool fan.'

Jack the ripper

Q. What's worse than getting raped by Jack the Ripper?
A. Getting fingered by Captain Hook.

Two testicles

Q. What did the left testicle say to the right testicle?
A. Dunno, but they were talking bollocks.

Two geeks

Two IT guys are walking through the park when one says, 'Where did you get such a great bike?'

The second IT guy says, 'I was walking along yesterday, minding my own business, when a beautiful woman rode up on this bike. She threw the bike to the ground, took off all her clothes and said, "Take what you want."

The second IT guy nods approvingly and says, 'Good choice – the clothes probably wouldn't have fitted.'

Women in heaven

Q. Why do only 10 per cent of women go to heaven?
A. Because if they all went, it would be hell.

Tragic threesome

A cruise in the Pacific goes wrong, the ship sinks and there are only three survivors: Damian, Darren and Deirdre. They manage to swim to a small island and they live there, doing what's natural for men and women to do.

After a couple of years, the previously chaste Deirdre feels so bad about having casual sex with two men that she kills herself. It's a tragic time, but Damian and Darren manage to get through it. They still have sexual needs and so, after a while, nature once more takes its inevitable course.

But a couple more years later, Damian and Darren begin to feel ashamed of what they're doing.

So they bury her.

Tommy cooper, R.I.P.

Q. How did Tommy Cooper die?
A. Just like that.

Middlesbrough pitch

They say the Riverside Stadium has the best pitch in the league.

Not surprising, when you think of all the shit that's been on it.

Die first

Q. Why do men die before their wives?
A. They want to.

Endless love

Q. What's the definition of endless love?
A. Stevie Wonder and Ray Charles playing tennis.

Beckham's skinhead

Q. Why did David Beckham have a skinhead?
A. Because someone told Victoria sex would be better if she shaved her twat.

Inflatable doll

A bloke goes into a sex shop and asks for an inflatable doll. The man behind the counter says, 'Normal or Palestinian?'

The customer says, 'What's the difference?'

The man behind the counter says, 'The Palestinian one blows itself up.'

Head stuck

Will Young, Robbie Williams and Kylie Minogue enjoy a night on the town together. After they leave the nightclub, Kylie's drunkenly mucking about when she gets her head stuck between some railings.

Robbie decides to take full advantage of this and lifts up her little skirt, pushes her thong to one side and gives her a good seeing-to.

Robbie says, 'That was great. Your turn, Will!'

But Will is crying. Robbie says, 'What's wrong, Will?'

Will sobs, 'My head won't fit between the railings.'

Baker's hands

Q. Why did the baker have smelly hands?
A. He kneaded a crap.

Cross the road

Q. Why did the man cross the road?
A. He heard the chicken was a slut.

Blair saved

Tony Blair is out jogging and accidentally falls into a very cold river. Three boys see the accident.

Without a second thought, they jump into the water and drag out the soaking Blair.

Blair says, 'Boys, you saved my life and deserve a reward. You name it; I'll give it to you.'

The first boy says, 'I'd like a ticket to Disneyland.'

Blair says, 'Certainly.'

The second boy says, 'I'd like an MP3 player.'

Blair says, 'No problem.'

The third boy says, 'And I'd like a wheelchair with a stereo in it.'

Blair says, 'But you're not disabled.'

The boy says, 'No, but I will be when my dad finds out I saved you from drowning.'

Jamie and a run

Q. What's the difference between Jamie Oliver and a marathon?
A. One's a pant in the country…

Cannibal

Q. What did the cannibal do after he dumped his girlfriend?
A. Wiped his arse.

Proof of identity

St Peter is standing guard over Heaven when a man approaches, claiming to be Bill Gates. St Peter asks for proof of identity, so Bill shows his bank balance. St Peter says, 'In you go.'

A second man approaches, claiming to be Stephen Hawking. St Peter asks for proof of identity, so Hawking explains the Big Bang Theory. St Peter says, 'In you go.'

A third man approaches, claiming to be David Beckham. But when St Peter asks him to prove his identity, Beckham gets annoyed.

St Peter says, 'Come on. Even Bill Gates and Stephen Hawking had to do it.'

Beckham says, 'Who?'

St Peter says, 'In you go.'

Bumpkin circumcision

Q. How do you circumcise a bloke from Norwich?
A. Kick his sister in the jaw.

Stuck to the floor

A woman's having a shower when she slips over on the bathroom floor. But instead of falling forwards or backwards, she slips sideways, does the splits and suctions herself to the floor. She yells and her husband comes running.

She says, 'I've suctioned myself to the floor!'

He tries to pull her up, but can't. He says, 'You're just too heavy. I'll go across the road and get a mate to help.'

He comes back with a mate, but, hard as they pull, they still can't get her off the floor.

The mate says, 'I've got an idea.'

His husband says, 'What's that?'

The mate says, 'I'll go home and get my hammer and chisel, and we'll break the tiles under her.'

The husband says, 'OK. While you're doing that, I'll stay here and play with her tits.'

The mate says, 'Play with her tits? Why?'

The husband says, 'Well, if I can get her wet enough, we can slide her into the kitchen where the tiles aren't so expensive.'

Chavs in a phone box

Q. How do you get 100 chavs into a phone box?
A. Paint three stripes on it.

Woman in the lift

A bloke walks into a lift and stands next to a beautiful woman.

After a few seconds he turns to her and says, 'Can I smell your knickers?'

The woman says, 'Certainly not!'

The man says, 'Hmm. It must be your feet, then.'

Twelve inches

Q. What's 12 inches long and dangles in front of an arsehole?
A. Tony Blair's tie.

Speaking to your wife

One bloke says to another, 'I haven't spoken to my wife for 18 months.'
 The other bloke says, 'Why not?'
 The first bloke says, 'I don't like to interrupt her.'

Women playing golf

Two women are playing golf. After hitting par on the first hole, they make their way to the second. Suddenly they hear a cry of 'Fore!', and one of the women gets hit on the head by a ball and collapses.

The second woman runs back to the clubhouse to get help. She cries, 'My friend has been hit with a ball. Can someone come and look?'

The nearest bloke says, 'Sure, where was she hit?'

'Between the first and second holes.'

'Well, that doesn't leave much room for a plaster.'

Women and hurricanes

Q. Why are hurricanes mostly named after women?
A. When they come they're wild and wet, but when they go they take your house and car.

Sperm count

An 85-year-old man goes to his doctor to get a sperm count.

The doctor gives the man a jar and says, 'Take this jar home and bring back a semen sample tomorrow.'

The next day the old man reappears at the surgery and gives him the jar, which is still empty. The doctor asks what went wrong.

The old man says, 'First I tried with my right hand, but nothing. Then I tried with my left hand, but still nothing. Then I asked my wife for help. She tried with her right hand, then her left, still nothing. She tried with her mouth and still nothing. We even called up the lady next door and she tried too: first with both hands, then an armpit and she even tried squeezing it between her knees. But still nothing.'

Shocked, the doctor says, 'You asked your neighbour?'

The old man says, 'Yes. And no matter what we tried, we still couldn't get the jar open.'

Laundry

Q. How do men sort their laundry?
A. 'Dirty' and 'dirty but wearable'.

Bondage-loving son

A mother is cleaning her 12-year-old son's bedroom when she finds a series of bondage and fetish mags.

She shouts for her husband to come and see.

She yells, 'What the hell am I supposed to do about this lot?'

The father says, 'I don't know, but whatever you do, don't spank him.'

Charlton suicide

A man distraught about Charlton's poor form prepares to hang himself. He decides to wear his full Charlton kit.

A neighbour discovers the body and tells a policeman. On arrival, the policeman quickly removes the dead man's Charlton kit and dresses the man in stockings and suspenders.

Baffled, the neighbour asks why.

The policeman says, 'It's to avoid embarrassing the family.'

Chav Eskimo

Q. What do you call an Eskimo chav?
A. An Innuinnit.

Sperm hold-up

A man wearing a mask bursts into a sperm bank holding a shotgun.

'Open the safe!' he yells at the woman behind the counter.

'But we're not a real bank,' she says. 'This is a sperm bank: we don't hold money.'

He says, 'Don't argue – just open the safe or I'll blow your head off.'

She obliges and opens the safe door.

He says, 'Take one of the bottles and drink it.'

She says, 'But it's full of sperm.'

He says, 'Don't argue; just drink it.'

She takes off the cap and gulps it down.

He says, 'Take out another bottle and drink it too.'

The girl drinks another one. Suddenly the bloke pulls off the mask and, to the woman's amazement, it's her husband.

He says, 'See? Not that bloody difficult, is it?'

Sick brothel

A bloke goes into a brothel with a tenner.

'Sorry, mate,' says the pimp, 'the only thing you can have for a tenner is a goat.'

The bloke shrugs, pays his money and shags the goat. The next week he returns to the brothel – but this time he's only got a fiver.

'Sorry,' says the pimp, 'but all you can get for a fiver is a peep show.'

So he goes into the peep show and there's a load of blokes spying on a guy wanking off a gorilla.

'Jesus,' says the first bloke. 'I've never seen anything like this before.'

'You should have been here last week,' says the bloke next to him. 'There was a guy in there shagging a goat.'

Queen's gift

Q. What did the Queen buy Camilla for her wedding anniversary?
A. A weekend in Paris and a chauffeur-driven Mercedes.

Bush in hell

George W Bush has a heart attack and dies. He immediately goes to Hell, where the Devil is waiting for him.

The Devil says, 'I don't know what to do. You're on my list, but I have no room for you. Tell you what: I've got some people here who weren't quite as bad as you. I'll let one of them go, but you have to take their place. I'll even let you decide who you swap with.'

The Devil leads Bush to a series of doors and opens the first. Inside is Ronald Reagan and a large pool of water. Reagan keeps diving in and surfacing, over and over again. Such is his fate in Hell.

Bush says, 'No, I don't want to do that. I'm not a good swimmer, so I don't think I could do that all day long.'

The Devil leads him to the next room. Inside is Richard Nixon with a sledgehammer and a huge pile of rocks. All he does is swing the hammer, time after time after time.

Bush says, 'No, I've got a problem with my shoulder. I'd be in constant agony if all I did was break rocks all day.'

The Devil opens a third door. Inside, Bush sees Bill Clinton, lying on the floor with his arms tied behind his head, and his legs spread-eagled. Bent over him is Monica Lewinsky, doing what she does best.

Bush stares in disbelief and says, 'Yeah, I can handle this.' The Devil smiles and says, 'OK, Monica, you're free to go.'

Redundancy

Mr Smith has two employees, Sarah and Jack. They're both extremely good workers. However, Mr Smith looks over his books one day and decides that he isn't making enough money to warrant two employees, and he'll have to make one redundant.

But he has trouble finding a fair way to do it. He decides to watch them work and the first one to take a break will be the one he lays off.

So he sits in his office and watches them. Suddenly, Sarah gets a headache and needs to take an aspirin. She takes the aspirin out of her purse and goes to the water cooler to get a drink to wash it down.

Mr Smith follows her to the water cooler, taps her on the shoulder and says, 'Sarah, I'm going to have to lay you or Jack off.'

Sarah says, 'I have a headache – can you jack off?'

Cross-breed

Q. What do you get if you cross a pitbull with a prostitute?
A. Your last blow-job.

Realistic vibrator

They've invented the most realistic vibrator yet.

Just before she has an orgasm, the vibrator comes, goes limp, farts and switches itself off.

Quiet night

Two married blokes are out drinking one night when one says, 'I don't know what else to do. Whenever I go home after we've been out drinking, I turn the headlights off before I get to the driveway. I shut off the engine and coast into the garage. I take my shoes off before I go into the house. I sneak up the stairs. I get undressed in the bathroom. I ease into bed… and my wife still wakes up and yells, "And what time do you call this?"'

His mate looks at him and says, 'Well, you're obviously taking the wrong approach. I screech into the driveway, slam the door, clatter up the steps, chuck my shoes against the wall, jump into bed, slap my wife's arse and say, "How about a blow-job?" And she's always sound asleep.'

Chav in a cabinet

Q. What do you call a chav in a filing cabinet?
A. Sorted.

Whores and bitches

Q. What's the difference between a whore and a bitch?
A. A whore sleeps with everyone at a party and a bitch sleeps with everyone but you.

Nursing home

A man puts his father in a nursing home. The old man cries, 'Please don't put me in there, son.'

The son says, 'Dad, I can't take care of you. I've checked the place out and it's the best there is. I think you'll love it.'

The next day the old man calls his son and says, 'Son, you were right! I love this place.'

The son says, 'Glad to hear it. What makes it so great?'

The old man says, 'Last night I was in my room and from out of nowhere I got an erection. A nurse came in, saw my hard-on and gave me a blow-job! I haven't had one of those in 30 years! I'd almost forgotten what it was like! It was fantastic!'

A few days later the old man calls his son again and says, 'You have to get me out of here. I hate this place.'

The son says, 'What's wrong?'

The old man says, 'Last night I fell down in the corridor. While I was still on my hands and knees, a male nurse came along and took me up the arse. I can't go on like this.'

The son says, 'Dad, I know that's terrible and we'll get it sorted out, but until then you have to take the rough with the smooth.'

The old man says, 'No, you don't understand. I get an erection maybe once a year, but I fall down two or three times a day.'

Jacko and a bag

Q. What's the difference between a supermarket bag and Michael Jackson?
A. One is white, made of plastic and should be kept away from small children. The other is used to hold your shopping.

Ukraine Y-fronts

Q. Why shouldn't you wear Y-fronts in Ukraine?
A. Chernobyl fallout.

Bite your breasts

A bloke walking down the street sees a woman with perfect breasts.

He says, 'Hey, would you let me bite your breasts for £100?'

She says, 'Are you mad?'

He says, 'OK, would you let me bite your breasts for £1,000?'

She says, 'I'm not that kind of woman! Got it?'

He says, 'OK, would you let me bite your breasts just once for £10,000?'

She thinks about it and says, 'OK, just once, but not here. Let's go to that dark alley over there.'

So they go into the alley, where she takes off her blouse to reveal the most perfect breasts in the world.

As soon as he sees them, he grabs them and starts caressing them, fondling them slowly, kissing them, licking them, burying his face in them – but not biting them.

The woman eventually gets annoyed and says, 'Well? Are you going to bite them or not?'

'Nah,' he says. 'Costs too much.'

Girlfriend

Q. What do you call a Norwich fan with a girlfriend?
A. A shepherd.

Jacko's pants

Q. Why are Michael Jackson's pants so small?
A. Because they aren't his.

Beckham and sperm

David Beckham walks into a sperm bank. He says, 'I'd like to donate some sperm.'

The receptionist says, 'Certainly, sir. Have you donated before?'

Beckham says, 'Yes, you should have my details on your computer.'

The receptionist says, 'Ah, yes, I've found your profile, but I see you're going to need help. Shall I call Posh for you?'

Beckham says, 'Why do I need help?'

The receptionist says, 'It says on your profile that you're a useless wanker.'

Acute angina

An elderly couple go to bed together for the first time. The old woman says, 'Before we start, I have to warn you that I have acute angina.'

The old man looks her up and down and says, 'Yes, and your tits aren't bad either.'

Pregnancy confusion

A man comes home one night, and his wife throws her arms around his neck and cries, 'Darling, I have great news: I'm a month overdue. I think we're going to have a baby! The doctor gave me a test today, but until we find out for sure, we can't tell anybody.'

The next day, a bloke from the electric company rings the doorbell, because the couple haven't paid their last bill.

He says, 'Are you Mrs Smith? You're a month overdue.'

'How did you know?' stammers the young woman.

'It's in our files,' says the man.

'What? Well, let me talk to my husband about this tonight.'

That night, she tells her husband about the visit and he, mad as a bull, rushes to the electric company's office first thing the next morning.

He yells, 'What's going on? You have it on file that my wife is a month overdue? What business is that of yours?'

'Just calm down,' says the bloke, 'it's nothing serious. All you have to do is pay us.'

'Pay you? And if I refuse?'

'In that case, sir, we'd have no option but to cut yours off.'

'And what would my wife do then?'

'I don't know. I suppose she'd have to use a candle.'

Condom emblem

The government today announced that it's changing its emblem to a condom because it more accurately reflects its political stance.

A condom allows for inflation, halts production, destroys the next generation, protects a bunch of pricks and gives you a sense of security while you're actually being screwed.